Y0-BEK-090

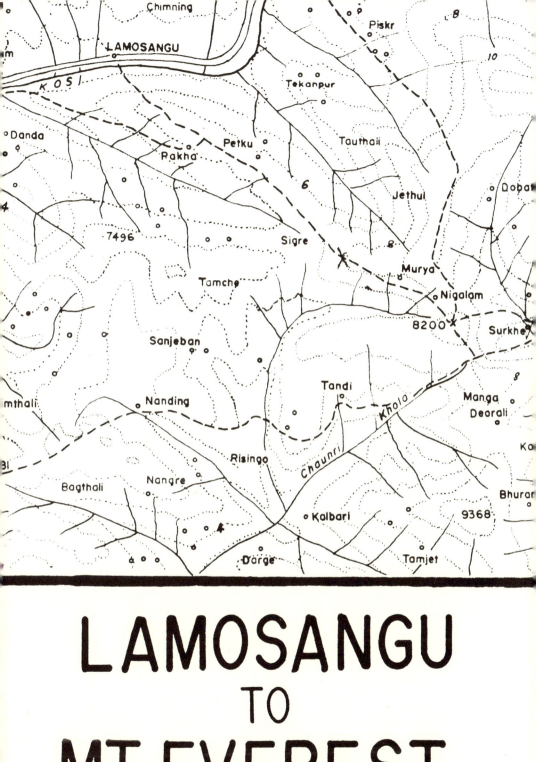

LAMOSANGU
TO
MT. EVEREST

miles 0   1   2   3   4   5   6

Scale: 1/2" to One mile 1:126,720

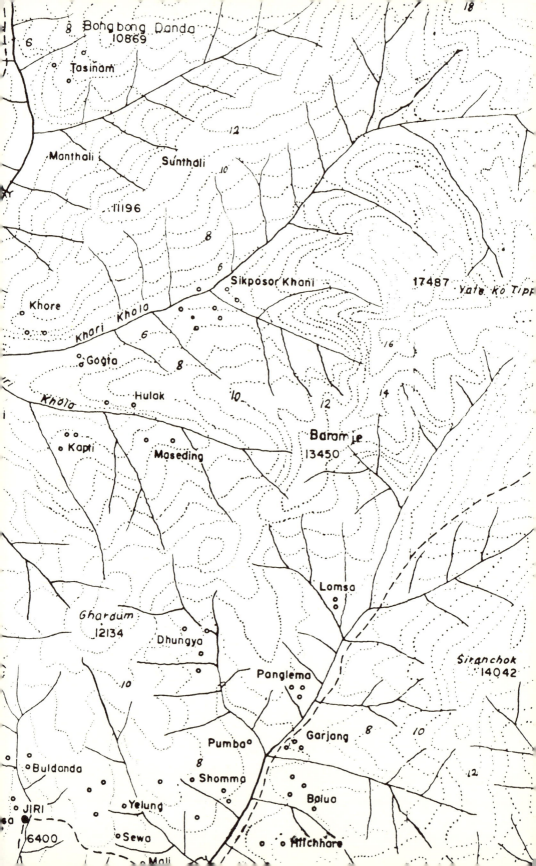

For Greg —
who devours the language
of our feet!

Bi—

10/92

TIME BY DISTANCE

poems by

William L. Fox

Windriver Series
Duck Down
Fallon, NV.
1985

Acknowledgements:

Thanks to the editors of *Chowder Review, kayak, Stinktree,* and *Three Rivers Poetry Journal,* who first published substantial parts of this book.

Cover design: Kirk Robertson

Photograph of the author: Barbara Hall

First edition of 500 copies; 26 copies of this edition have been lettered and signed by the author.

ISBN: 0-916918-28-9
ISBN: 0-916918-29-7 (Signed Edition)

Library of Congress Catalog No.: 84-70842

Publication of this book has been assisted, in part, by receipt of a grant from the National Endowment for the Arts, a Federal agency.

Copyright © 1978, 1985 by William L. Fox
All rights reserved.

A Windriver Book

Duck Down
P.O. Box 1047
Fallon, NV 89406

I have friends who won't walk a trail twice. They cover ground fast, talk little, and look for a different way down the mountain. I go along. But at times I prefer to track back on myself. The territory behind is new, transformed by time as well as distance.

In the fall of 1975 I retraced a route thru the Eastern Himalaya, which I'd first walked and written about a year and a half before. Not only was I trekking thru country I knew in advance, but poems too. There was a line for every step, a poem for each place. It took awhile to shunt memory far enough aside to let in the new views.

I wrote poems everyday on that first trek in 1973, but nothing during the second except a letter home.

The first poem here is a reminder of how we travel: multiplying to ourselves each day how far we've come by how far we have yet to go. It's a curious calculation that applies to cars and airplanes as well as feet.

The second series is of distance — literal and chronological poems from '73. I've often been asked to add in print the stories between the poems, tales of misadventure I tell when reading these in public. But the stories belong in the air, alive to each occasion. I save that backtracking for the oral, hoping the reader will get to the poems, not shunted aside by narrative.

W. F.

for U Tsering

Thyangboche   Dingboche   Pangboche
      Pheriche   place place   the
map   is always   right

Nuptse   Lhotse   Phortse   Kharte
      Khumbila   Kunde   Khumjung
place place   the map   is always right

Pemba   Pasang
      A Gelu   Ang Geljen
of people   the map   makes no mention

Time By Distance

MULTIPLICATION

we lay the watch on
a map and divide
distance over time

we say at this rate we'll
never get to lunch or
it's a long walk to camp

we take the
length of stride
the length of day

we use the sun
the watch and
our stomachs

after the first week
it's always the same
no division but
an easy multiplication

speed by time and
how much ground
this will cover

how fast can
we walk and
for how long

all this in
terms of legs

legs are not
what we remember

after a month it
is always the same
for those who last

time by distance
we say
how many days
by distance

how much 35 days
of 350 miles
can be

this is the table of memory
a larger addition than
rate of motion for a body
from a starting place

and this 12,250
is what we travel.

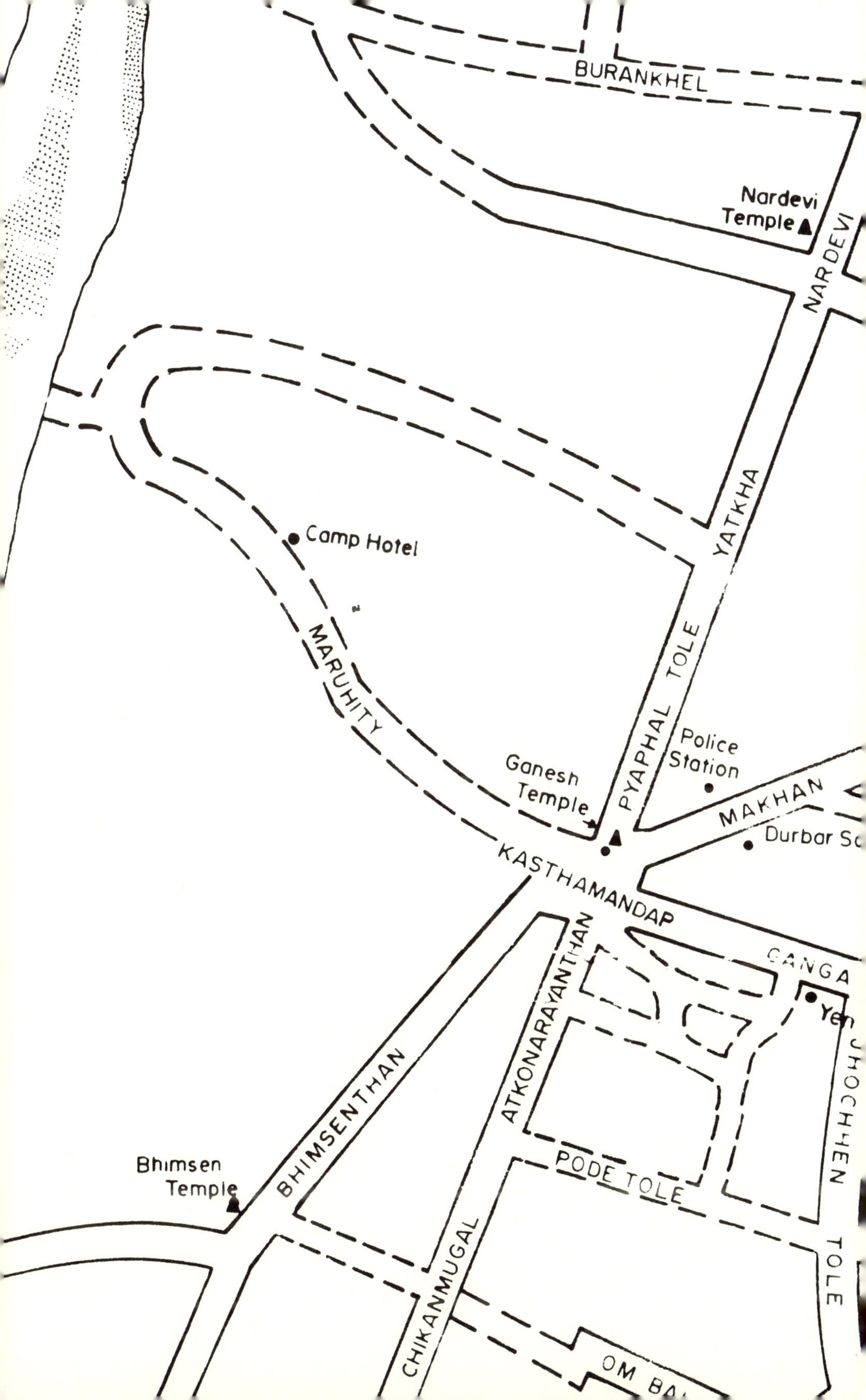

BURANKHEL
Nardevi Temple
NARDEVI
YATKHA
Camp Hotel
MARUHITY
PYAPHAL TOLE
Police Station
Ganesh Temple
MAKHAN
Durbar Sq
KASTHAMANDAP
GANGA
Yen
ATKONARAYANTHAN
JHOCHHEN
BHIMSENTHAN
PODE TOLE
TOLE
Bhimsen Temple
CHIKANMUGAL
OM BA

KATHMANDU

white and simple
as a fence
        the peaks frame Kathmandu

pale and naive
our legs
        in long trousers

                *

the cloth shops
all together
        a street hung
        inside out

                *

when the bamboo scaffolds
are taken off
the temple
        just another pagoda

but for now
a jigsaw
of workmen

                *

on the hill
looking down a line
of Hindu shrines
    one is a baboon!

        *

at a corner
the pungency
of urine
has attracted
even you

        *

nine at night
on the largest avenue
a policeman's harmonica
    heard two blocks away

        *

next morning
a rooster appraises dawn
    we too have counted
    all night long

on the floor
our packs
tight as sleeves
rolled up to muscle

SILDUNGA

our first tent
pitched in a field

the farmer plows
up to our feet
        and turns

his bullock shadows
the whole tent

so tired
we could be
turned under

YARSA

aspirin

she is as patient
with us
as with the flies
on her broken hand

downstream her mill
grinds bone with grain

THOSI

rooster

downstairs in the hay
an orange wing shouts Fire

for this house the light
is never out

SETI

our six blue tents with
eight nylon lines apiece

wind invents a tune
on forty-eight strings

*

the lama is unwell
but leaves his window open

downstairs his housekeeper
folds up her arms
for the night

*

prayer wheel

inside a square room
the barrel chest of Buddha
hangs from the ceiling

swings an inch or two

who has just left
with me in the only door?

LAMJURA PASS

and still
prayer flags
on the pass
point south
frozen in
the north wind
mani for thaw

JUNBESI

the skinned goat
is all stomach
the stomach all grass
still green

*

everyone else is
asleep when we
cross the river
to get drunk

we must rouse
half the village
to find some chang

but in the end
even the children come

*

the dancers hold together
thump   thump   thump   thump
a stock of logs end up
thump   thump   thump   thump
a floating loggerhead
my thumps are all wrong

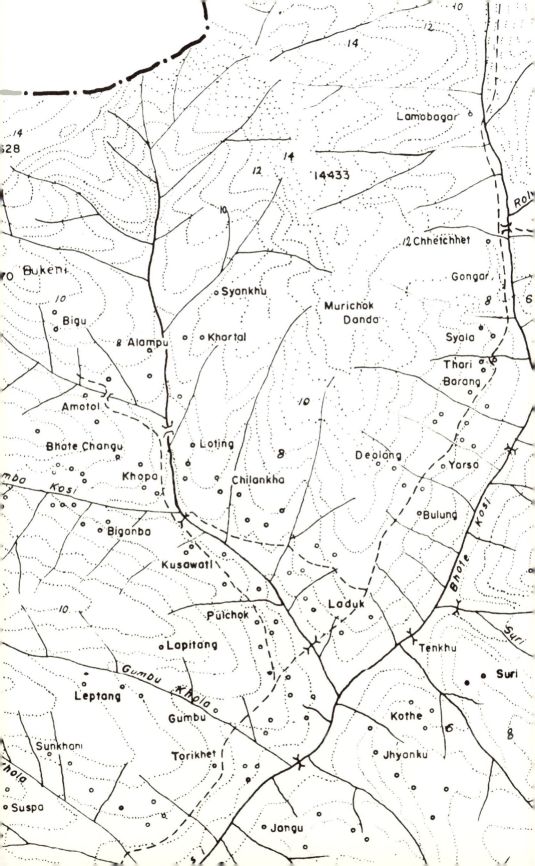

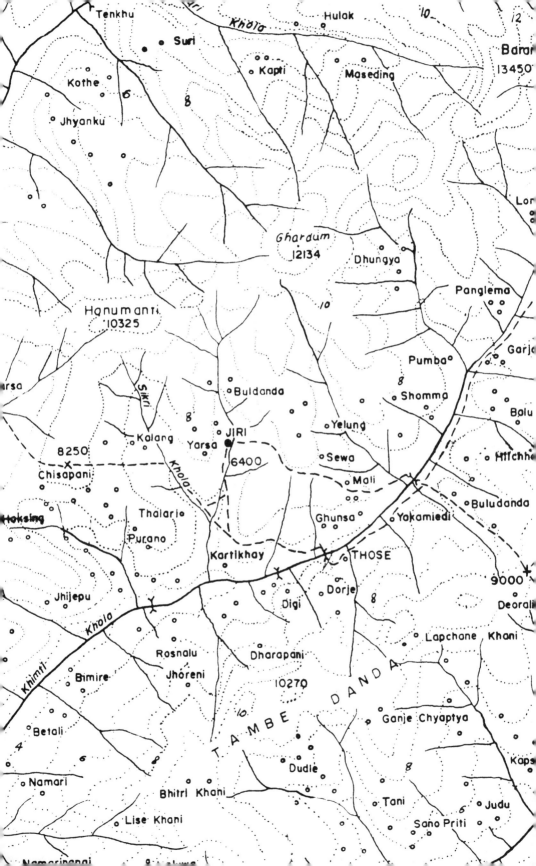

ABOVE JUNBESI

Everest!
there's the snow plume

next to your cameras
and long lenses
my poems squint

DUDH KOSI

cold and opaque
the corpse of a snake
belly up
in the gorge

CHAURIKHARKA

too far ahead
i walk alone
thru the village

my back is a boulder
carved in mani

two women in a field
scratch for potatoes

mostly stones
they throw
over their shoulders

i sit on a rock
and wait for the cook

everyone follows
his basket of pots

*

and Lukla airstrip above
is on the lost plateau

        planes drop straight
        from Hollywood

        the icy peaks
        close up their circle

the old fuselage
on the runway
a dinosaur

NAMCHE BAZAAR

when we return
two weeks from now
the waterfall
across the valley
will still hang frozen

two new shops
will sell tinned fruit

KUNDE

step over a rock fence
and the field
bursts into doves

      the houses look up in surprise

stones and doves

*

at my tent door
Ama Dablam looks down
its nose of ice

*

a whirlwind hits camp
two tents
burst into threads

      the shutters of the village
      are white

that night
safety pins
on every flap

*

after the party
we knocked down
a wall

drunk polar bears
rebuilt an igloo

all locked out
by the safety pins

KANETEGA

this is the wall
the wind hits
that makes the earth
go round

THYANGBOCHE

unsure if i
may walk thru
the gateway

a monk comes down
and offers wine

*

at the monastery
front stairs
are forbidden
but to the left
another door
where even Sherpas
must stoop

a low doorway
for humility

*

inside the temple
the faces of Buddha
peel off the wall
gay smiles
of curling paint

*

the courtyard
filled with firewood
no room for
dancing in the snow

*

the roofs held down
by stones
even so close
to heaven
     and still
     the monks
     have work to do

*

Breitenbach

on the ridge
no room
for another grave

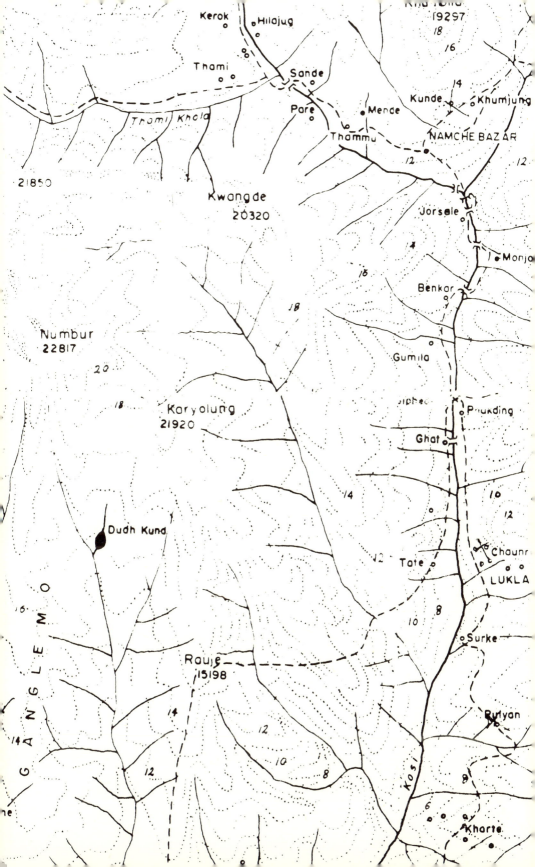

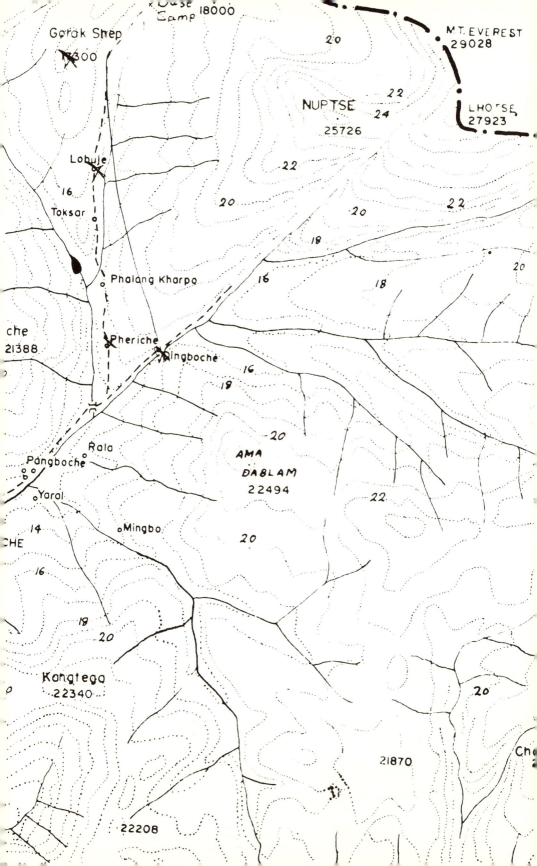

PHERICHE (14,000 ft.)

a leg
goes to sleep
too soon
an arm pretends
it isn't there

the body deserts
nerve by nerve
and the mind sticks
to any metal thing

LOBUJE (16,000 ft.)

two hundred unnatural yaks
sit on your pack

all the way to Lobuje
the fragrant trail
of two hundred more

*

every now and then
the one breath
that keeps the lungs
from collapse

GORAKSHEP (17,000 ft.)

where is the warmest
    sleeping bag
    who gets
    the extra socks

who cooks tonight
    and how
    does a zipper work?

*

someone coughs in camp
    snow leopard
    hunting up the weak

KALA PATTAR (18,000 ft.)

alone above camp
as high
as you've been
as high as you need

    the horizon tightens
    around your head

    *

Everest tomorrow
will be clear

but now
with a few clouds
i see the way up

THYANGBOCHE AGAIN

blood pheasant
cross the trail
downhill to water

my friend and i
say nothing
     the rest
     see nothing

*

in the printmaker's room
even the eye of the fire
waters in its own smoke

lean out the window
and look left — Everest

from soot and
rice paper
prayers to hold back
the view

*

leaving

the heels begin to go
because you land there first
then the sole thins out
a landslide begun years ago

shoelaces pass thru
like emigrant worms

the intricate fingers
of daylight lace up

the old uppers open
their chapped lips
and drink up sweat

a little water
for the trail
a bit of salt
for good luck

CHAURIKHARKA AGAIN

the farmer hasn't yet
repaired our hole
knocked in his wall

even the crows know
everyone goes thru twice

*

Sherpa woman

her braids solemnly
cross themselves
no no   we will not
undo ourselves

PUIYAN

the monkey eats an orchid
thirty feet above camp

we have little to offer
after that

and yes
he leaves
without any of us noticing

PANGUM

once more we
come back drunk
in the dark

     and cross three streams
     too many

next morning
the trail disappears
for miles
beneath wet leaves

     *

in the rain
one thouand steps
cut in stone

at the top
the pass is
shoulder-wide

the clouds
back up behind me

SANAM

at the valley head
wood chips
add smoke
to fog

around every bend
the beat of an axe
counts my steps

      the woodcutters and i
      dream at the same pace

*

we camp in the trail
the only flat spot

sick in my tent
everyone trips over us

*

behind the monastery
there's no one
tho everyone
goes there

*

that night
my tentmate goes out

thru our open flap
the Milky Way

i am lost

ARUN KOSI

from one watershed
to the next
like the peak
of a roof
  crossed with one foot
  then the other

   *

bathing in the river
so much water
we can never use

taken off guard
my soap floats away

floating after it
on my back
the first raindrops
   *

at breakfast
a dead cow
rolls downriver
  stiff legs
  snap on rocks

   *

Ghurka

a drunken soldier
marches on the beach
his grey moustache
at right shoulder arms

the parade never rests
          or is at ease
but salutes itself
at each step

a regiment of footsteps
follows in the sand
          the moon folds up
          like a flag

          *

fireflies fly ahead
of their own distraction

          *

jackals won't cross
the moonlit bridge
and howl

the cables shiver
and throw silver crosses
on the water

          *

after lunch
a green lizard
falls out of a tree

so he too
must be sleepy

*

Rai Family

strapped across his back
a dull tin wing

wife and children
each grasp a corner

every breeze
threatens divorce

he crabs sideways
up the trail
nose to the grinding wall

in the first monsoon
they'll all go mad
under the new
tin roof

HILE

how many times
we've unrolled our tents
in a monastery courtyard

*

at three a.m.
horns and drums
for one minute

        chanting monks
        float thru a break
        in the clouds

        *

i sit on a bench
in morning fog
    a friend stops by
    to rub my bare knees

DHARAN

the trails unwinds
like a clock
and strikes pavement

the last bridge
gives under no one
and the bounce
in our step
backfires

> the terai
> holds nothing back

*

in the bazaar
drunk at dusk
for the last time

shops close up
the street
loses its face

only the silversmiths stay
to hammer out
a signal

BIRATNIGAR

flying back to Kathmandu
the mountains are overcast

the rivers we crossed
wash down our tracks
and spread them on the plains

walking, anywhere

for Stan

if i drift downtrail and
you touch my elbow
we'll change path

there's always a gap
an opening between trees
a low spot in the wall

NOTES:

page 23:   "mani" — prayer

page 24:   "chang" — millet beer

page 28:   "Dudh Kosi" — milk river

page 36:   "Breitenbach" — an American
            climber killed on Everest in 1963

page 52:   "Rai" — Nepalese lowland tribe

page 54:   "terai" — jungle flatland

William L. Fox was born in 1949 and has lived in Reno since 1960. His previous collections of poetry are *Iron Wind* (Sono Nis Press, Canada), *Trial Separation* (Caveman Press, New Zealand), *Election* (Three Rivers Press, Pittsburgh), *Monody,* (Laughing Bear Press, Seattle), *First Principles* (Future Press, New York), *The Yellow Pages* (616 Center One Press, Reno), and *21 And Over* (Duck Down Press, Fallon). He is currently Executive Director of the Nevada State Council on the Arts and editor of West Coast Poetry Review Press.

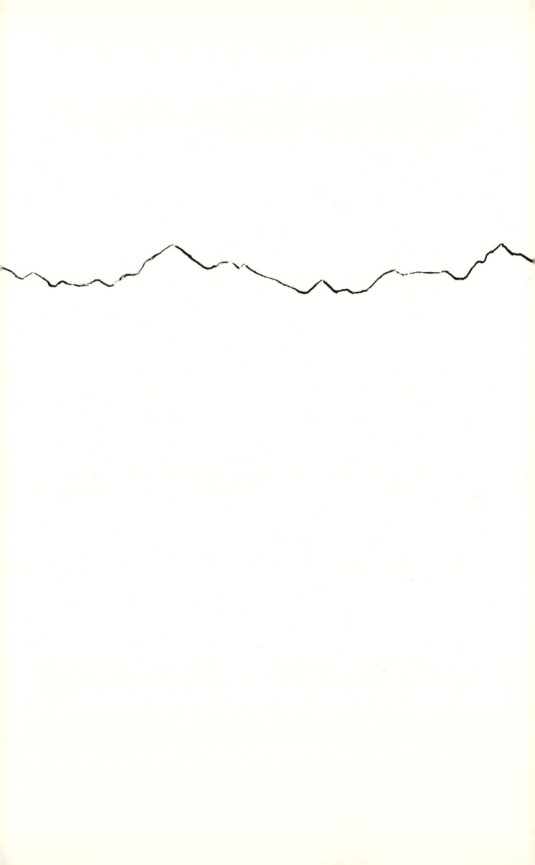

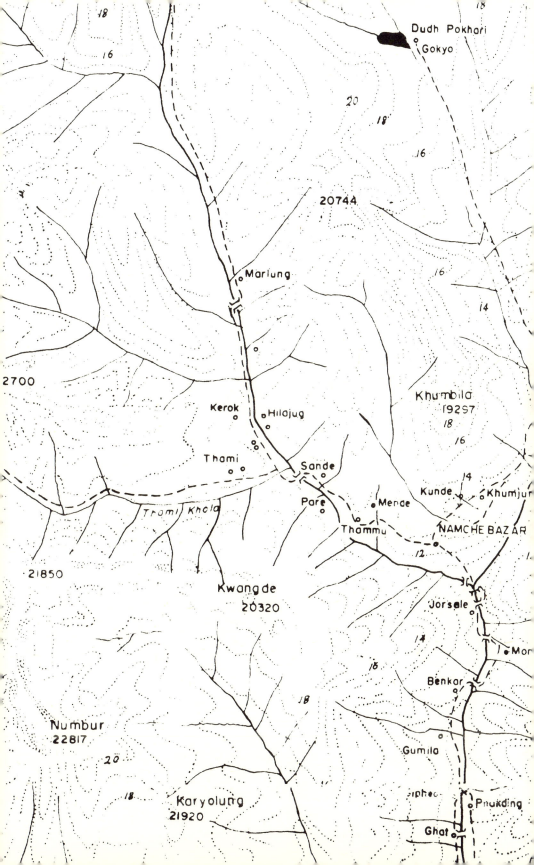

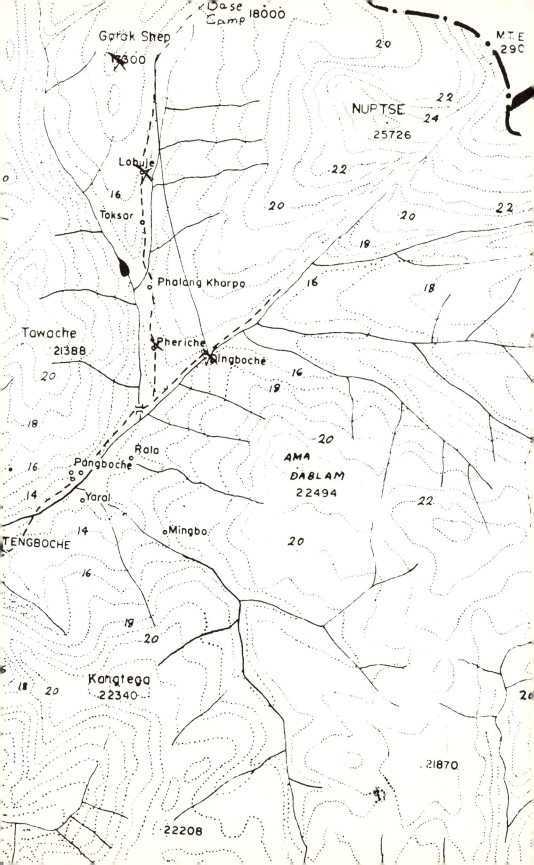